# Don't be a
# Jelly Donut

*BY*

**CARLEEN ROBERTS**

ISBN: 979-8-9878824-0-5

Author: Carleen Roberts

Book Cover Design: Provision Multimedia Group

Photography: NJR 2 Photography LLC.

Printed in the United States of America

# Forward

I know by now you are saying to yourself, "Why would I want to be a Jelly Donut?" Or "Who would want to be A Jelly Donut out of all the donuts in the world?" Lol! You'd be surprised how many of us are already exemplifying the characteristics of a Jelly Donut. Hopefully, by the time you are finished reading this book, you will fully understand how some of us demonstrate the contents of a Jelly donut.

### Thank You!

First, I'd like to thank my Lord and Savior, Jesus Christ, who is my All in All. I could not have gotten this far without Him, and He gets all the Glory! Thank you, Lord, for being a true Father to me.

# Dedication

I am dedicating this book to my husband, who is the optime of a true Man of God. I am grateful that I do not have to look outside our home for an example of true Love and Godliness. You are the Priest of our Home.

I love you more than words can express. Thank you for pushing me to write this book. Thank you for believing in me and seeing me far beyond where I could see myself. Thank you for taking my little thoughts and making them Big. Thank you for laboring with me when things got difficult on my journey. Your voice made me stand tall in places where I wanted to quit, in something I didn't want to do, and in front of the enemy who fought me daily. You are forever my greatest Pusher (outside of God). Your Love and Walk with God kept my heart upright and provided the example I needed on this journey. Your hand of excellence covered me when I wanted to be messy and directed me back to God. Your Love superseded judgment. Thank you for your covering, your prayers, and your consistency in making sure I didn't revert to being a Jelly Donut. 😄 🖤 I am grateful to have you walk side by side with me. Thank you for loving me the way that you do.

-Forever is not long enough. Love you, Babe. 💕

# Table of Contents

# Chapter 1

## A Jelly Donut's Choice

**M**any of us might not want to be something, but by default have become the very thing that we did not want to become. It might have come from the influence of our circumstances, environment, or a traumatic experience that we have gone through in our life. Sometimes we indirectly become what we are comfortable living in. Our physical and mental capacity could have limited our exposure to more or less. For instance, if we were raised Catholic since birth, most likely when we become adults, that is the road we will choose because we weren't exposed to anything else. It has been within us since birth, and we weren't given a choice. Usually, it's our parents who choose for us. We might have chosen a different religion to follow if we had been given an option, but because of the influence of our environment, it was a choice we made within ourselves. We acted upon it. It was no fault of our own. If we don't know, we aren't accountable. It is only that which we do know that we become responsible for.

We all have been guilty of it at some point. We have walked into things that were decided for us without having any input or influence on the decision. Some of us discover it early on. Others find out later in life. Some of us never uncover it. However, once we become aware, it is at that point that we must decide which road we will take. The one that was chosen for us or the one we will choose. It's just that simple. We have to be very decisive in whatever we decide to do, or else we will follow what others want us to do. We follow others when we don't have our minds made up. It creates imbalance, instability, and double mindedness. Our answer has to be firm and solid so that our motives, moves, and mindset will be. We must leave no room for anything to try to sway us in another direction outside the direction God has given us. When God puts something in your heart, the feeling will be so overwhelming that you can't shake it, no matter how hard you try. It appears in every area of our lives: dreams, conversations with strangers, books, signs, our spirit, etc. Do you know how some people say it feels like a gut feeling? It's very similar to that. That is God's way of getting us to act on the decision He has already made provision for. All He needs is our YES! Everything else is on the other side of that.

I think it's interesting how God chooses us, but He gives us a choice to choose Him. Why did He make it an option for us to select Him? Why didn't He make it our decision to choose Him? Even in choosing Him, our decision must be SOLID. That's why He never wants to force Himself on anyone. Why? Because once we decide to select Him, every decision we make moving forward will include Him. He wants us to have a SOLID foundation. Therefore, it requires a SOLID answer. Our choice matters! If He didn't give us a free choice, some of us would give the excuse, "well, I didn't choose You; You chose me." God wants us to choose each other. He is a faithful husband. God doesn't wish to have mistresses. He wants companionship. Those who have decided to be with Him and Him alone. Have you ever heard, "when you know better, you do better?" Once we make a choice, we become accountable for that choice and the knowledge we gain from it. Choosing Him makes us better! It's just like a marriage. You become responsible for one another and the knowledge you gain while being married to each other. Oh, the wisdom in that!

What if a jelly donut had a choice? Would it have chosen to be covered in powdered sugar or Chocolate glaze? Would it have chosen to be filled with a specific type of Jelly? Maybe Strawberry Preserves or Grape Jelly even. Unfortunately, it doesn't have a choice. It will become what others want it to become. The influence, opinion, and creativity of others will determine how significant the Jelly Donut will be. What about you, who has a free choice? What will you decide, or will you let others decide for you? Will your greatness be depended upon what other people think you should be? Who will you serve, and will it be your choice? It's your decision. Choose wisely.

*"And if it is evil in your eyes to serve the Lord, choose this day whom you will serve, whether the gods your fathers served in the region*

*beyond the River or the gods of the Amorites in whose land you dwell. But as for me and my house, we will serve the Lord." -**Joshua 24:15***

# Chapter 2

## Where do Jelly Donuts Live?

I know people who are genuinely donut lovers. They only go to certain places to get donuts and go to local bakeries, local donut shops, grocery stores, etc. After taking a poll and speaking with a few of them, I discovered that they chose certain places because they enjoy the product's taste. They also love the service each location provides. The taste and the service had the most significant influence on their choice. This discovery let me know that where the donut lives determine if that donut gets a visit.

If the local bakery was our choice, that is where our donut lives. We have become satisfied with where it lives based on the taste and service that the place provides. We are okay putting in the effort or purchasing it because of where it Lives. It's all about the location! Where we live matters! Out of all the places we could have chosen, we chose specific places because they satisfied our desire.

When I say where we live matters, I am not referring to our physical place of residence. Where does our soul reside? Where does our mind reside? Where does our heart reside? They should all reside

11

in the same area, which is in God. When we live in God, and he lives in us, we don't mind tasting and seeing He is Good. We are okay with going the extra mile to serve His people. When we get a taste of the Lord, we wouldn't want to live anywhere else. It's an experience and a residence that cannot be put into words and something you will never encounter elsewhere. A visit with Him changes everything. If you have visited Him and things are the same, you were at the wrong place. It is the same with those who have chosen our favorite Donut Shops. It was the taste and experience that made us choose those places. It can't be compared to another. It satisfied our desire. When God lives in us, He meets all of our desires. He said he would give us the desires of our hearts. He does it so graciously!

When we live in God, we provide service to Him, and he becomes of service to us. It's a mutual benefit. We go to our local donut shop for the taste and service of their product. We benefit from them. They benefit from us because we provide a service to them by paying for their product. It's a mutual benefit! The difference here is that when God lives within us, He pays the price for us, and for anything that He desires us to have, He provides the provision for it to be paid. He takes care of all of our needs. Nothing left undone! It is truly an experience that will change your taste, appetite, and life. He is our All in All.

Jelly donuts live in many places. Some donuts live in a local donut shop. Some live in bakeries. The disturbing thing about that is that it can change by the week. One week it could be here and not there and vice versa. There is no telling where it might be next week. The decision does not belong to itself; therefore, it has to live wherever it is placed. The jelly donut is not stable. You could go to the donut shop tomorrow and they might not have your type of donut. That forces you to have to look somewhere else for it. Its place of living might have changed. The place where God lives never changes. We can surely depend on Him to be stable. What about you? Where do you want to LIVE? Do you want to be tossed here or there like that of a jelly donut? Do you want to LIVE where your foundation is solid and cannot be moved even if the enemy tried to move you? Our decision to live in God creates a solid foundation for our life and those connected to us. We should know where we LIVE and who lives in us at all times. When we decide to live in God and He in us, we cannot be moved unless we forfeit the territory. We have to give the adversary permission ourselves. We have to make the right decision. We must Live in God and allow Him to Live in Us. It is crucial for our destiny!

*"Neither shall they say, Lo here! or, lo there! for, behold, the kingdom of God is within you. -LUKE 17:21*

# Chapter 3

## White Powdered Sugar

To be quite honest with you, I used to dislike Jelly donuts. Mainly because of its covering. The Powdered white sugar was just too much for me, especially since I am a little OCD and can't take the mess. The covering is quite messy and gets all over the place. (ugh!)

One of the places that I frequent to get donuts is my local donut shop. For some reason, they always have the Jelly Donuts covered in White Powdered Sugar. Just imagine trying to grab a cup of coffee in the morning before work and grabbing a White Powdered Jelly donut along with it. You may not make it to work clean due to the covering on the outside of the donut. If you had chosen another type of donut, you might have had a better chance of staying clean. The covering is our choice. Powdered Sugar or No Sugar? It's ultimately our choice.

Our choice in covering matters. It matters because it determines how clean we will become from the inside out. When we allow God to protect us, no matter how messy we become outside, he cleans us up. When we have no covering or become outside of His covering, we are left to clean up our mess which can make things messier! I know firsthand. I have been there. I thought I was helping and was making things worse. We must remove our hands and allow the hand of God to take complete control. His covering is our security. It secures our life no matter what comes our way when we are under His covering. We are under His care. We are under His guidance. We are under His protection. We are under His leadership. We are under His direction. Even if we decide to step outside of it, that still, small voice shows up like a siren reminding us that we need to get back in place asap. He will always warn us by signs before we become entangled in anything that will cause us harm. The Holy Spirit never leaves us ignorant of the enemy's devices. We must obey those signs rather than ignore them. It will help us greatly in the end.

Jelly donuts do not get to choose their covering. If they are covered in powdered sugar, it was what someone decided to cover them with whether they wanted to be covered with it or not. The care and cleanliness of the donut is determined by how it's handled by the person who decides to take care of it. Why? Because it doesn't have a mind of its own. Someone or something chooses everything about its being for it to remain a donut. When people have control over us, they control our thoughts and motives. Too often, we put our hearts and minds into other people's hands. We, in turn, become what they want us to become rather than what God put inside of us to become. Why do we give them that much control? We should not put them before God. Who have they become to us? We never want their desires to become more significant than God's desires in our life. If so, it places them above God. Our word tells us that He is a jealous God, and we don't want Him to be jealous. It might not be too pretty!

Without having a mind of our own, the world begins to toss us to and fro, and we begin to cover ourselves with the things of this world instead of the things of God. We began to wear this world and make decisions based on what it wants us to be or become. Nothing is covering us to shield us from the deception of what's attached to those things. Look what Adam & Eve did when they walked outside the covering and disobeyed God. They began to cover themselves up with this world, and because they allowed the world to cover them, they became subject to the world. The world had infiltrated their minds, and it touched everything about them.

It's almost like a Jelly donut and all the messy white powdered sugar. It gets everywhere as soon as you touch it. Have you ever tried eating a powered Jelly Donut? As soon as you touch it, it gets everywhere. I remember when I was driving and eating one. It got it on the steering wheel, the gear shaft, and the mirror. It was on everything that surrounded me! It didn't clean itself. I had to clean it all up. It's the same with the things we touch or get into when outside God's covering. The adversary tries to connect to our loved ones, minds, hearts, careers, dreams, etc. It comes trying to strip us of everything that God said we could have, and guess what? He leaves us to clean up the mess he made!

I remember when I was doing my own thing, my way, thinking I was going to get away with it. I didn't believe for a second that it would touch my children since they weren't doing the actual act of what I was doing. I should have included the spiritual aspect of it. Well, honey, let me tell you! It was showing up in my children, who weren't with me when I tried to do it. However, because they are connected to me and were in my surroundings, the affliction touched them too. It showed up in their behavior. It scared the mess out of me! I quickly began to get myself together because I didn't want them to get hurt because of a wrong decision I had made. Our sin begins to touch our surroundings whether we want it to or not. Once we invite it in, it comes to do collateral damage. We must remember that it's a spiritual fight attached to our destiny.

Just like a Jelly donut, the things we do outside of the covering of God will try to afflict those close to us since we've allowed the enemy exposure to it. It tries to touch everything! When we are outside of God's covering, we are exposed to many things, and the enemy feels as if he has free reign. When you are covered, he might get close, but nothing he tries will work! At some point, he will realize that Jesus is our covering and nothing is more powerful than He is. Satan will think twice about trying to come that way again. God will surely handle your battles. Why? Because He has you covered, and your battles belong to Him when you are covered.

Don't be Like a Powdered Jelly Donut. They have a messy covering because they didn't have a choice, and this world chose the covering.

Choose God as your covering and allow Him to show you your purpose. Allow Him to show you Who and What you shall Be. His covering is sure, and it is Solid. Make a Sound decision to be Covered by Christ. You will not regret it!

*PSALM 91: 1*-16-*He who dwells in the shelter of the Most High will abides in the shadow of the Almighty. I will say to the Lord, "My refuge and my fortress, my God, in whom I trust." For He will deliver you from the snare of the fowler and the deadly pestilence. He will cover you with His pinions, and under His wings, you will find refuge; His faithfulness is a shield and buckler. You will not fear the terror of the night, nor the arrow that flies by day...*

# Chapter 4

## Jelly Donut Etiquette

I am a firm believer that actions speak louder than words. There have been too many occasions in my life where people said things but did not follow through with them. I would be so upset. If I took their word, I trusted them to see that word through. I trusted them with the handling of my heart and the belief that we agreed with each other. I opened up to the idea of their word, and they would see it through. Frequently, I was let down. It goes back even to childhood. Before getting delivered from rejection, those moments would sting quite a bit. Those experiences caused me to hold grudges, isolate myself, and put-up complex walls for people to overcome. My heart wasn't handled correctly, and in turn, it caused me to mishandle others through my pain indirectly. It wasn't on purpose, but because of the fear of being hurt again, I wouldn't allow people who could adequately handle my heart in my space. It caused me to miss out on so many great relationships.

We must stop allowing people to mishandle our hearts! They must be always handled with care. We must make it a habit to protect our heart's posture. We are often very loose with allowing others to hold our hearts or touch them in ways God didn't design them to be touched.

There are no etiquette classes or books to teach you how to handle or eat a jelly donut properly. You learn how to manage from your own experience. My first experience could have been smoother. Due to it being my first time, I didn't grab extra napkins or buy anything to drink with it. My donut was also covered in a heap of white powdered sugar, so you can imagine the mess made while eating it. Honey, there was more powdered sugar on my pants than in my mouth. It was also all over the steering wheel, seat, and dash and even got in my hair. After all of that eating, I was very thirsty. What a mess it was! Lesson learned. It was my first time, and I had yet to experience what eating a jelly donut would include. I didn't know how to properly handle it because I wasn't experienced in learning how to handle eating one. Once I purchased more jelly donuts over time, the less mess there was and the better I became at eating them. I've mastered it now. Haha!

Some people don't know how to handle our hearts properly because they aren't experienced handling a core of our magnitude. Some of us could be "too much" for people (in a good way). They can't handle our success, decisions, or personality, and that's okay. There will be someone who can handle us properly and has become experienced in handling our hearts with care. Perhaps the person only knows how to handle toxic people. They might have only had experience with handling tainted hearts or environments. That's okay too, but that person is not for us. We want to be handled by someone with experience in treating and managing people with care. God has someone just for you. That's why I love God even more. Even if we go to Him with our toxic, messy, and broken hearts, He can mend them. God is a master at handling things with care.

Most of the time, we know when someone cannot or is unwilling to handle us with care. We allow people to handle us still. The signs will be there. Again, God will not leave us in the dark. Allowing people to mishandle us creates mistrust, walls go up, and we tend to hold grudges. All of this makes an unhealthy heart posture. Our hearts were pure before the Lord when He created us. We must do our best to ensure that it maintains its original intent. Allowing people to tamper with our hearts by being deceptive or dishonest can cause us to become bitter. This behavior could cause us to become resentful toward them, but also toward others who are entirely innocent. We must maintain a pure heart posture, which means we must be mindful of those handling our hearts.

When I ate my jelly donut for the first time, it was not with care, and there was a mess everywhere! The same thing happens when we allow people to mistreat us, abuse us, deceive us, hurt us, etc. The situation becomes messy! That's what the enemy wants us to do. He wants us to give him the authority to hurt us. We are the ones who have to open up a portal to permit him to do so. God never intended for us to be in pain. His original intent was for us to be loved and appropriately handled without pain. When He created us, it was with care. Every atom of our being was thought of and put together strategically. We were created in His image and likeness; therefore, He made us in His perfect image. Every hair is in its proper place! Why? Because He cares about everything concerning His people. It shows His concern for us. It shows us the wisdom, time, and detail He put into creating us. It is our responsibility to take care of and maintain what He made.

Please ensure that the next time you get a Jelly Donut, you manage it with care. Grab some napkins. No mess!

*Isaiah 46:4,* *GNT I am your God and will take care of you until you are old and your hair is gray. I made you and will care for you; I will give you help and rescue you.*

# Chapter 5

## Dwell like the Dozen

I f you have a big family like me, you must get a dozen at a time when you go get donuts. Especially since you can't go home with white powdered sugar all over your mouth, you'd be in big trouble if you didn't bring any back for everyone else. Hahaha!

Usually, I have to purchase a dozen and ensure that the dozen includes the donuts that everyone else likes. Of course, we all don't like the same donuts, and some of my family like blueberry, glaze, Boston crème, etc. God forbid if I go home and don't have one for everybody. Whew!

What I love about the dozen is that they put them all in one box. (12) different types of donuts all in one box, yet they all dwell together. The glazed donut isn't worried about the jelly donut getting powder all over it. The Boston crème donut isn't concerned with getting chocolate on the blueberry donut. You probably said to yourself, "jelly donuts don't talk," but you get my drift. Lol!

23

How come we all can't get along like the dozen? We all have different personalities, shapes, sizes, fillings, colors, etc. We are who God created us to be. I love opening up the box and looking at all the different varieties of donuts. They all have different tastes and provide different eating experiences. Likewise, with us as a people. Can you imagine if God created us all the same way? What a boring life that would be! No type of color in life. Just blah! He made us all different because we all have our purposes. My purpose might be to speak. Someone else's purpose might be to write. When brought together I can talk about what they have written. Their book gets exposure, and we both walk in our purpose together. It's similar to the different types of donuts for my family. My husband might like the glaze, and I like the Boston crème. Each donut serves a purpose, but All are satisfied in the end.

As a people in general, we need to be able to dwell like the dozen. Dwell together in unity like He called the church to do. This is why we all have different gifts. What if we had all singers and no drummers? What if we had all ushers and no preachers? Everybody brings their contributions to the House of God, and we work them together in unity. Unity glorifies God; believe it or not, it satisfies our Souls. One body compactly jointly fit together - Ephesians 4:16. We cannot have one person doing everything. It will become a chaotic body, and people will be unsatisfied. There is a corporate reward that God designed for us all to receive. The condition is that we have to dwell together in unity. No gift is greater than the next—God's design for us all to walk in our purpose individually and collectively within His body. Allowing each other to exercise our gifts and walk in our purpose promotes unity and oneness in the body. I'm sure God would be pleased. We would be the beneficiaries of all His goodness!

Let's dwell like the dozen. Even the (12) disciples stayed together despite their differences. Nevertheless, they stayed together to fulfill the purpose of Jesus' walk here on Earth. We are different in many ways, but we are ONE in God.

Let's strive to Dwell like the dozen!

*Behold, how good and how pleasant it is For brethren to dwell together in unity! It is like the precious oil upon the head, Running down on the beard, The beard of Aaron, Running down on the edge of his garments.* **-PSALMS 133:1-3**

# Chapter 6

## Make me A Donut

I remember being younger, and people would ask me, "What do you want to be when you grow up?" That question was the opener for many little children growing up, especially when conversing with adults. It was also one of the opening questions as part of the school activity. Most of us have been asked that question sometime or another in our life. As I grew older, I wondered if those who asked even cared. I found myself answering that question over and over again, but my answer was the end of the conversation. There needed to be a follow-up or discussion about how to get where I wanted to be. There was a nod in agreement or a follow-up question when they disagreed with my answer. Often, as a child, when they disagreed, I almost felt pressured to be what they wanted me to be, but as an adult, I am changing that narrative.

Many of us have goals and aspirations we desire to achieve, but I wonder how many of us consider the process it takes to get there. A Jelly Donut does not just appear on the Shelves of the local Donut Shop. There is a process that has to happen before the donut is made. There was a lot that went into making it; the concept, the shape, the

26

ingredients, the color, the audience, the demographics, and more. Many things have to take place before the idea even enters the factory. As a child, I wanted to be a teacher. However, I didn't know you had to go to college at that time. I was surprised to find out that my college years depended on the type of teacher I wanted to be. I also needed to be made aware that there were grade levels, different types of education degrees, etc. All I knew was that I wanted to do it. I hadn't even thought about the process it took to get there.

We have to understand that everything has a process. EVERYTHING. Great ideas take time to happen. It takes time. It takes effort. It takes prayer. It takes meditation. It takes sacrifice. It takes consistency. It takes a made-up mind. It takes courage!

I'm sure the person who created the Jelly Donut didn't just throw something together. I'm sure that the process was a tedious and strenuous one. Yet, the results prove that a great work ethic went into the idea. We cannot give up during the process. We have to push even beyond the limits that we set for ourselves. When we write the vision and make it plain, pray over it, and walk in it. We must understand that we work within God's limits, not our own. Knowing this alone will help us succeed! I remember starting MWCC, and in the beginning, it was going ok. During the process, when I was about knee-deep, all hell broke loose. I was mentally drained and physically ready to fight any and everybody. I knew God told me to start MWCC, and the enemy knew it too, which is why he tried to get me to quit at the very climax of the process. There were times I would have to get on and encourage others while I needed to be encouraged. There were times when I was afraid because the background noise of others had gotten so loud, and their words seemed to mean more than God's word. Sometimes I couldn't eat because my mind and thoughts were all over the place. One day I realized that God told me to start, so why was I worrying about finishing? All I needed was His word, and He had given it. Whatever God provides us with a vision for, He makes provision for. I kept praying. I kept fasting. I kept in constant communication with God, and He prevailed! The process was complicated. Very hearty and tedious, but I felt God had more, and He did. I got the Victory, and He got the Glory!

Our response to the process determines the outcome of the product. The job of the adversary is to stop God's plan. He will always try to put a seed in our ears to get us to shut down. It starts in your ear. Your ear is the portal to your senses that controls your thoughts and filters what enters your heart. We've got to learn how to shut the negativity down immediately when we hear it. I remember having to remove myself from certain things to protect what my ear heard so that it wouldn't take seed form. We must defend our Peace by what enters our ear gate. How many of us have acted off of something we heard and haven't even seen yet? That's because what you heard took form before seeing it. That's the enemy's job to put a "bug" in your ear to get you, not ever to see where God wants to take you. He did the same thing to Eve in the beginning. He put a bug in her ear, and it took seed form. Don't take the bait. Pray, Push, and Press. Refrain from negating the process.

The process of making a jelly donut and the process of you becoming what God has ordained aren't the same process, but the point is that it takes time and a heart to go all the way. Every process is different. It's ok if someone else's operation finishes sooner than yours. Your product might carry a heavier weight. That's a word in itself! Be ok with your process. Good, bad, or indifferent. Own it and go all the way. Some doors are waiting for you to enter through. God is with you every step of the way. When you get there, Remember to bring the donuts!

*"Be strong and courageous. Do not fear or be in dread of them, for it is the LORD your God who goes with you. He will not leave you or forsake you." **Deuteronomy 31:6***

# Chapter 7

## No Donut Left Behind

Writing this book has catapulted my mind into a donut frenzy. I started researching and learning all about Jelly Donuts. I mean true donut knowledge overload. Lol! However, I am intrigued by all that is happening with a little ol' Jelly Donut. They've put some thought into making it unique. When you look deeper into finding out the truth about a matter, you'd be surprised by what you discover.

In my research, I've found out that there is a sure way the donuts have to be kept when they aren't being used (or eaten). They can become molded if they aren't stored properly (especially dairy-filled and jelly-filled donuts). Usually, dairy-filled donuts go rancid at room temperature and have to be refrigerated immediately after about 2-4 hours of sitting. The store temperature matters for those donuts to last. If any are leftover, they must be put in a sealed container and refrigerated. If this process is not followed correctly, this could be costly for the owner. He loses profit and could lose customers if served while molded. It must be preserved perfectly for the use of the product to be maximized. The goal is to get all of the donuts off of the shelves. The importance of how the donut is kept is more significant than how it is sold.

Look at God! How you keep yourself while waiting on God is more important than you getting to your destination. My God! Why? Because when we get there, we must be able to KEEP what God has given us. If we don't discipline ourselves in the wait, when we get to our destination, we could put ourselves in jeopardy of losing everything!

Often, we get frustrated with the wait. We cannot let the weight of the circumstance determine how we wait. Weight vs. Wait! The weight of what we are going through is not more substantial than the strength God gave us to wait. We have to ensure that we are waiting in God while waiting on God. We must do it! Otherwise, we could lose our cool, tongue, and all we've already completed. Waiting in God provides security that ensures the wait will be worth it no matter what happens during the process. Even when we don't see or hear God, we still have to wait with great expectations. The adversary wants us to think that nothing will happen, we won't succeed, and we will fail. The truth is God is working behind the scenes to make ways for things to happen. When we think He isn't going to do it, He shows up. That is why we mustn't lose ourselves in the wait. We preserve ourselves by praying, fasting, reading, adhering to God's word, and being obedient to His instructions. We can't get bratty and act like spoiled children who have tantrums. You will find out quickly that

31

those behaviors won't work with God. You will mess around and fall out and hurt yourself.

If those jelly donuts aren't appropriately preserved while waiting for someone to purchase them, they will be no good to anyone. They will be thrown out! The way they are kept while waiting determines their maximum use, which is the same for us. The way we wait determines how our gifts can be maximized. The way we keep ourselves in God while waiting determines if we can maximize the gifts of God within us. I don't know about you, but I want God to use every gift He has put in me to its total capacity. I don't want a drop of gift left in me when I leave this Earth.

My friend, don't let the Weight of this World stop you from waiting correctly in God. Don't be like the old moldy donuts that get thrown out. I can't imagine God wanting to throw any of His children away. Even the Donut store owner tries to do everything he can not to have to throw away the product that he put his time, effort, and money into. God put His all into us, and He wastes nothing! Wait patiently. Wait with courage. Wait while listening. Wait while obeying. Wait with Understanding. Wait while praying. It's not about what you are waiting for that matters, but how you wait determines what you shall receive.

No donuts left behind!

*But they who wait for the Lord shall renew their strength; they shall mount up with wings like eagles; they shall run and not be weary; they shall walk and not faint.* **Isaiah 40:31 ESV**

# Chapter 8

# Donut Holes

S everal times, I ordered donuts from Dunkin when we would have parties at work. I would usually order (2) dozens of donuts. However, I noticed that there would always be donuts left over, so I started purchasing the mini donut holes after that. If your favorite Donut place is Dunkin Donuts, they give you this cute little box with mini donuts. I liked the smaller box versus carrying (2) big boxes. Lol! I quickly noted that no mini donuts were left after the parties, and they would all be eaten!

In writing this book, the vision of that came to mind. It made me think about the Bigger Donuts vs. the Mini Donuts. I observed that both donut boxes had the same product; it was just that the portions were smaller in the box of mini donuts. I couldn't understand why people still ate the same product but preferred smaller portions over larger ones. In my head, it's the same donut. If I eat (5) mini donuts, that would be equivalent to one big donut. However, the lesson in it is this.

There are no mini donuts. Literally! When I would buy them, they'd be gone. In this world, we have some cruel people, and sometimes, if they have the bigger things in life, such as houses, cars, careers, status, etc., they tend to try to belittle those who don't have those things. You have to understand that God does not look at what's tangible and can be brought. He looks at our hearts. We see that God uses people who seem to have little in the eyes of this world but who have a heart for God. With that, they have everything! There are no mini-gifts! They are all Great in the eyes of God.

So often, we compare ourselves to what others have, criticize ourselves, and beat ourselves up to no end. We have to stop doing that. The word even tells us that it's not wise to compare ourselves to those who think highly of themselves. We need to find out the depth of their story. When we envy their things, envying their process accompanies that. Just like some people desire the more considerable portion over the smaller amount, your portion might differ. Though it seems smaller in weight, the depth of your portion might carry more. God doesn't think as we do. Look at Hannah's portion. Her adversary (Peninah) had way more children than she did. The Lord always gave Hannah a Worthy portion. Worthier than all Peninah had. Her portion carried more weight because she was faithful to the portion God gave her. I'm sure Hannah felt inferior, humiliated, less of a woman, and many other things, but her portion was Worthy and acceptable unto the Lord. There is nothing "mini" about the portion God gives us.

Know who you are. Know who you belong to. Knowing who you are goes to great lengths when the adversary tries to convince you that what God has for you isn't enough or is "mini." His word alone is More powerful than any two-edged sword. The enemy better ask somebody! Our God is no coward and no wimp. We serve a Great and Mighty God. Some call Him Jehovah. Others call Him El Shaddai. Many call Him the Prince of Peace. We have to use His word to fight back. Don't take down and let anything minimize what God called you to. You are Great in Him!

The adversary always wants us to think that we aren't anything because he knows God's portion is Worthy. God told us that greater is He that is within us than he that is in this world- 1 John 4:4. The enemy keeps pressuring us because if we believe it, he knows he's in trouble. Believe it. You are a child of the King, which means you were born Great. Step into it.

No More Mini Donuts!

*"One who is faithful in a very little is also faithful in much, and one who is dishonest in a very little is also dishonest in much." -Luke 16:10 ESV*

# Chapter 9

## Surprise Fillings

T he very first time eating a jelly donut, I was upset. Very upset! So much so that I never wanted to eat one ever again.  Now, that might seem petty to you to stop eating jelly donuts, but I had a good reason why! Well, in my head, I did. lol

I am not necessarily a jelly-filled type of person. Meaning I'm not too fond of anything with filling in the middle. I wouldn't say I like cherry tomatoes unless they are cut because I don't want the filling bursting in my mouth while eating. I don't want any surprises. I don't like chocolate that's filled with cherries or anything that's jelly-filled things that have fillings in the middle. I usually stay away unless I like it. Part of it has to do with needing to know all the specifics about the filling. Is it thick, runny, solid, bitter, or sweet? All these things matter to me because of how they affect me inside and outside. Will it agree with my stomach? If I bite too hard, will it mess up my clothes? I think about all of this. As a person with a busy schedule, these things matter to me. I need to be productive at all times without interruptions. One wrong move could affect my entire day.

Now back to my first jelly donut experience. I was driving, and I remember biting into it as I would bite into any other donut. That was a mistake! With a Jelly donut, you have to be careful how you bite it because the jelly will come spilling out of nowhere if you aren't careful. Guess what? It did, right onto my white-pressed shirt. I was hot! I was so surprised that it was filled with that much filling, and it came out on the side that I didn't expect. I expected it to come from the middle and not from the side. I knew it was filled, but I didn't realize the magnitude of the filling. I felt unguarded and unprotected, lol! You'd be surprised how one Jelly filled donut can ruin a morning. I wasn't ready!

Have you ever expected someone to be a certain way, and they weren't? You thought they were one way, and it turned out that they turned out to be something else? I can guarantee you it was because of how they appeared to be outwardly rather than what they were inward. Who people seem to be inwardly, speaks volumes. It speaks well over the outward appearance because the heart cannot see. The heart doesn't see color; it doesn't see race; it doesn't see a status. It just simply loves what it loves without condition. Whatever is in a person's heart will appear in their actions. Sometimes we miss the mark because we go by word, not action. What is the heart saying? It's always proven through action. The word tells us that out of the heart flows the issues of life.

We go into relationships seemingly ready to receive people at the surface, thinking we have seen who they are. Once you dig in, you will find that it isn't what you expected, and the remnants of who they genuinely are fell on you. It's almost like preparing yourself for a relationship. You practice cooking, praying, cleaning, patience, understanding, etc., and the person doesn't receive any of it. They appeared to be the type of person to accept you as is, but when you discovered who they were inward, there seemed to have been a block in the connection. This is a huge warning sign! So often, we connect with the flesh thinking we are connected spiritually until we find out that our spirit man keeps rejecting the connection because it's not divine. Two hearts cannot become one if one of the hearts isn't connected to God. It has to be a heart connection and not a head connection. It will never work. Have you ever been with someone you can agree with on a meal but not something in the Spirit? Some people might decide in the flesh but not in the Spirit. It can happen, and we can misconstrue this with a spiritual connection. However, the Spirit will never lead us wrong and will always send out warning signals when danger is near. Adhere to the signs to avoid any surprises.

Some connections leave you a mess to clean up. Unfortunately, the remnant of that mess seems to linger sometimes. We must ensure that we are cleaned up of the first mess before proceeding to the next relationship. That topic is for another chapter. It happens to the best of us. We will only know how to overcome a thing if we experience it. I would only know how to prepare to eat a jelly donut if I hadn't first experienced the mess with the first Jelly Donut. That experience prepared me to do better preparing and eating it the next time I got one.

We often get into messy situations, and we begin to question if God is even in them. In some cases, He is. He is trying to prepare us for what He has ahead. Yes, your relationship might have hurt like hell, but it provided lessons, wisdom, and discernment for the next relationship. You will be able to identify those issues immediately. There won't be too many surprises this time. You will know what to expect, how to react, how to speak, what to pray for, and what to look for. Some surprises are alright. These are lessons that the Lord uses to prepare us to master that which He has given. Some of us wouldn't know how to recognize a good husband if we hadn't dated a few bad men. We also must understand that some experiences also pull underlying issues out of us. Have you ever thought you weren't this way or that, and you met someone who brought terrible things out of you? You see, God wants us to get all those things out before reaching our destinations. Sometimes that means being put in certain positions to know who we are and are not. God wastes nothing! Even what the enemy meant for our bad turns out for our good.

Yes, my first experience eating a jelly donut was a pretty messy one. Yes, I was upset because my outfit was ruined. Yes, I needed to prepare for all of the filling. Yes, I was frustrated, but that lesson taught me much about my next experience. Not only has it prepared me to be ready for what it did to my outside but also my inside. You can guarantee that I was fully prepared the next time I got a jelly donut. I had wet ones, and I made sure I didn't have my Sunday's best on and didn't dive in to eat it aggressively! I also ensured I didn't eat it with coffee to avoid a quick bathroom break. The next time I got a jelly donut, I ate that donut like a lady! It Won't happen to me again. No, ma'am, no ham, no turkey! I am now a professional jelly donut eater. Hahaha!

The Lord is not surprised by anything. He knows all. When we communicate with God, we minimize being surprised by the enemy's tactics. He doesn't leave us ignorant of the enemy's devices. He always warns and prepares us. We have to adhere to the signs rather than override them. Proceed with care and caution. I sure did the next time I ate a Jelly Donut. No more surprises!

*"We must pay the most careful attention, therefore, to what we have heard, so that we do not drift away." -**Hebrews 2:1***

# Chapter 10

## Somebody has to make the Donuts

Whenever I enter a Donut Shop to get a donut, I rarely think about who made the donuts. My focus is to get in and get out as quickly as possible, and I am usually always on my way somewhere and only have a little time. Have you ever thought about that? Have you ever said to yourself, "I wonder who made the donuts?" or are you like me? In and out!

I don't think the donuts flew on the shelves. Somebody had to make them, right? They didn't just get there by themselves. Do you ever think about where you are and who went before you to allow you to be there? Think about it. Your grandmother might have gone through some things in her life so that you wouldn't have to go through them. Your mother might have broken some barriers so that you could walk through doors that were closed for her. Whenever we get to a particular place in God, we must remember those who have paved the way for us to be where we are. Never take it for granted!

We don't know how much pain, struggle, time, and effort it took for them to push so that you could have providence. We always have to be grateful for their lives and the work they put into ensuring our future. I think about some of the things my grandparents and even my mother went through that I didn't have to. I wouldn't have made it out of some of the things they made it out of. I appreciate what they did for me by honoring them in how I live. I also think about what my leaders went through and did so that I would be able to properly divide the word of truth and share the gospel with other people. It took a lot of courage and effort, mainly because I was hard-headed. Hahaha!

It's just like the jelly donut. Someone put work into ensuring that we could have our donuts when purchasing them. They might have had to stay overnight or All day to get it ready just for us. Appreciate those who went before you. God always knows who to use for what. He knows who to put on the job because they will complete it successfully. We have to Remember their labor of love in our time of triumph. Keep them in prayer, bless them, and give honor where honor is due. The best way we can honor someone is by the way that we live. It shows them that their living and labor were not in vain. It shows them that you care and that what they went through wasn't in vain. Nobody makes it by themselves. There is always someone who has helped us along the way. I thank God for the people he has put in my path. I had many people who prayed for me. Many people encouraged me and pushed me along the way. It helped a great deal when things got heavy. Remember those people. Honor them. God sent them.

` Somebody has to make the donuts!

*Honor all men. Love the brotherhood. Fear God. Honor the king. -1 Peter 2:17*

# Chapter 11

## Sugar Rush!

I haven't met one person who doesn't like donuts. If you are that person, shame on you! Live a little. Hahaha! Although many people love donuts, some people can't have them, and for some reason, we always want what we can't have. It's the lust of our flesh.

I can recall a time when I was visiting some relatives of mine. As usual, there is always food involved whenever there is a gathering of us. Every type of food you can imagine. One of my relatives was a diabetic, and although we were all aware of this, it didn't keep us from refraining from keeping the sugary items away from them. This particular time, we had donuts. Of course, their favorite donuts were there, and they couldn't resist. The enemy always puts things that will tempt us in our way. Everybody else was going about and not paying the relative any mind. Everybody was enjoying themselves. Since we were all grown, we didn't feel the need to have to babysit anyone, but Maybe we should have. We could have paid a bit more attention.

As time passed, one of my cousins noticed several donuts were gone, but we didn't make a big deal out of it since there was still enough left for us all. As the night grew fonder, we realized that this relative was not feeling well. I'm laughing now, but the first thing we tried to give them was ginger ale! I don't know why we think ginger ale soothes everything, but that didn't work. Later we found out that this relative ate (4) donuts. They just had to have what they weren't supposed to, and it almost cost them their life. Their sugar levels elevated to the point of hospitalization for several days until they could get it regulated. We were all scared at the time and in panic mode. See what happens when we can't have what we want, yet we still do it?! We have to have self-control. She knew she wasn't supposed to have one donut, let alone four. Why do we always have to do the absolute most? One needed to be more. That's how the enemy works. He always wants us to overdue what we aren't supposed to do. He always wants us to do it in excess.

How often has God warned us not to do something, yet we still do it and expect Him to bring us out of it? How do we do something without counsel with God and then want to take counsel once we get into trouble? It doesn't work that way. We have to take counsel before the action, not after. We have to be obedient to God's voice and His word. We have to include Him in everything we do. Otherwise, we risk our lives and all that comes with the risk we have taken. I can imagine the pressure my relative was under with all the sweets right in their reach, but even then, we have to overcome temptation by exercising Self Control. No matter how close of reach things are. The enemy will always put extra pressure on you to do the wrong thing. Did you ever notice that he doesn't exercise this same pressure when it's to do something good? Never! It's always when he wants us to put ourselves in harm's way. Learn to Deny him and deny your flesh. Everything that looks good is not suitable for us. Some of us have found that out the hard way. Be obedient. We know what we can and cannot have.

Most of the time, the things we aren't supposed to have only last for a while. It took a good minute or two to eat that donut. That little time cost them days in the hospital and affected their health. The donut was the bait. Everything else they went through was connected to that. The enemy always wants to try to rush us into doing something terrible. When we do, it pushes us into the hurt and pain of that choice. What the enemy offers is never free. It costs us, and we have to pay for it with pain. Pain is the interest in what we take! Listen to God's voice amid temptation.

We must also be mindful of our sisters and brothers' weaknesses. After that incident, it made me wonder if we hadn't had the donuts there, would they have suffered the way they did? Would their sugar levels have elevated? If we know our sister struggles with something, don't be a stumbling block for them to fall into that temptation. For instance, if we see our brother struggling with fornication, don't invite him to a singles event. We might cause him to fall into that sin. We don't want that blood on our hands. We have to look out for one another. Be mindful of our surroundings to avoid falling into the devil's traps. If there is a trap set and one of my sisters or brothers is aware, I want to know about it, so I don't fall. We are our sisters and our brother's keepers. We have to do better at ensuring that we are all made aware of the enemy's tricks and plans. God is pleased when we operate in a spirit of Unity.

No more sugar rushes!

*"I say then: Walk in the Spirit, and you shall not fulfill the lust of the flesh. For the flesh lusts against the Spirit, and the Spirit against the flesh; and these are contrary to one another so that you do not do the things that you wish." -**Galatians 5:16-17.***

# Chapter 12

## Dressed Donuts

You have probably realized that my favorite donut spot is my local donut shop. If you live in New Jersey, you know what that place is. Haha! I thought I was living until my son started working at another donut shop, and it was a fancier donut shop that I hadn't experienced before. My donut life shifted, or so I thought.

The donuts at my usual donut shop were plain compared to the ones where my son worked. The first time my son brought donuts home from his job, I could barely see the donut. They looked like donuts from a gourmet donut spot. One of them had bacon with some glaze on it. Before touching the donut's surface, you had to bite through all of that. I have to admit the donuts were good. The donut shop he was working at had many different toppings. My local donut shop doesn't offer a large variety of toppings.

I remember he brought a blueberry donut home from work. It had some lemon topping on it, but once you get past the topping. The blueberry donut tasted the same as my local donut shop's plain blueberry donut. All of the toppings can fool us, if we aren't careful. Sometimes things aren't what they are all dressed up to be. I am not knocking the place where my son worked. The donuts are delicious. They have a specific audience for their product. I'm trying to help us to understand that everything is only sometimes as it seems.

As people, we judge a book by its cover. Especially when we think people are of a certain status. We think because they have the marriage, car, house, etc., they've got it all together. They appear to be all dressed up, but under the surface, they might be someone different. We need to get to know people in spirit, not flesh. Sometimes people camouflage themselves in what they wear and have on the outside, but deep down, they are dealing with some issues within themselves. Our first assumption of people can never be based on how they appear on the outside. Who are they inside? We find this out when we try the spirit by the spirit. For example, I learned what the basic blueberry donut tasted like because I first tried my local donut shop's basic blueberry donut. When I tried the blueberry donut where my son worked, I knew what I was tasting because I had tried it before.

When we have tried the Spirit of God before getting involved with people, we know what His Spirit gives off and what the results of being in His presence does for us. When we come in contact with people and try His Spirit by theirs, the results should be the same. The aroma that they give off should be the same. This prevents us from getting into hurtful situations. When danger is near, the Spirit of the Lord will send sirens that you can't ignore! Adhere to the warning. As soon as I bit the blueberry donut from my son's donut shop, I knew I had tasted that same taste before. God will not leave you ignorant of any situation.

We are all human. Being all dressed up and appearing to have it all together doesn't Separate us from the trials of life. I'm not saying that there are people who don't dress well and act well because there are plenty who do. However, no one is better than the next. We all have extraordinary abilities in our Unique Way. The dressing doesn't make a person; it just makes an appearance of who that person appears to be. No matter how many toppings we try to add, a donut is a donut. Once all of the toppings are removed, a donut will appear. Who are we without the dressing? At the end of the day, we will be who and what God says we are. Dressing or no Dressing! These worldly things do not make us who we are. We can't take any of it with us when we go. Who we are is determined by what's in our hearts, not what's in our hands. Be aware of the dressing. Try the spirit by the spirit. It will never lead you astray.

*Beloved, believe not every spirit, but try the spirits whether they are of God: because many false prophets are gone out into the world. 1 John 4:1*

# Chapter 13

## Donut Vibes

I rarely go into my favorite donut shop, and there isn't a line. Some days I am ok with it, but those are usually the days I am not rushing. However, on the days I am rushing, it's pretty annoying, lol!

To make you aware, all the folks in the donut store when I go are my donut friends. They don't know it, but I do. Lol! They are because we all have one thing in common: we love donuts! So I've taken it upon myself to make them my friends whether they like it. Haha! In all seriousness, they are my buddies, and sometimes when I am rushing, I become upset with them. They have no idea that I am until I get inside the store. Have you ever been rushing and become mad at every driver, every person before you in line, and the slow cashier? Are you upset because you need to get somewhere fast, and it seems like everybody is slowing you down? This happens when I go into the donut shop, and the line is out the door. Not only that, but the young lady in front of me seemed to be ordering food for the entire office, and her order is taking longer than usual.

Meanwhile, I am behind her in line, huffing, and puffing, throwing out a few "OMGs," and waving my hands in the air. 😄 She has no idea what my problem is; now her energy shifts because mine has. I was the only one who knew that I was in a rush. Everyone else is oblivious to my issue. Because they are unaware, they are just carrying on with their day as usual. How are they supposed to know without me verbally telling them that I am running late? The vibe and energy I was giving off were already speaking negatively, and she would have to guess or wonder what my issue was. Have you been there?

We have to be very intentional about our energy and our speech. Unfortunately, everybody is not a prophet, nor do they have glass balls that they carry around daily to try to figure out our issues. We must understand that our energy shifts atmospheres, and we must be careful not to shift it in the wrong direction. It is imperative that if we are having a personal issue within ourselves, we have to deal with it personally. It is not meant for the multitude to be a part of or take part in that issue. It's our issue that we have to confront. The root of the problem was that I woke up late. Again, my donut buddies have yet to learn that I woke up late. They also didn't know this wasn't my first time doing it. It just so happened that the line was longer than usual this time, which sent me into an attitude frenzy.

Had I dealt with the root of the problem beforehand, they wouldn't have had to be in contact with the negative energy I was giving off. Here this young lady is in line, minding her business, ordering her food, and I am behind her with all this negative energy. My energy, in turn, shifted her energy. She became combative with the cashier, forgot a portion of her order, and was upset with me. Negative energy! It has a way of spreading like wildfire. Who do you think God will charge if she goes to work and has a bad day? Right. Me.

We have to be mindful of what we give off. It matters. Sometimes we use the excuse, "that's just how I am," or "they already know me." That might be true, but it is a cowardly excuse. God is also aware and wants us to change some of our ways. We have to be approachable. Do you know that some people have what we need and want to give it to us, but because we need to be more approachable, they won't even attempt to provide it? It's our negative disposition and energy. I had to check myself. There have been several people who told me that they didn't think I liked them. I was totally in shock! I thought I was the most approachable person until I had that donut shop visit with the long line. Lol! There were some adjustments I had to make inwardly. We are citizens of the kingdom. Our disposition should always represent such. No one wants to deal with someone who is always negative and expects the world to know what they are going through. As people, we must do better and be intentional about the energy we give off. Be nice to your donut buddies!

*13 That energy is God's energy, an energy deep within you, God Himself willing and working at what will give Him the most pleasure.* **-Philippians 2:13-23**

# Chapter 14

## Tea or Coffee?

I Was not a coffee drinker until my good sis (no names mentioned, lol) got me hooked on a place that starts with an "S". 😄 They need a separate line for people that need deliverance in the drive-thru. I'd probably be in the deliverance line every week. Pray for me. 😵

I wouldn't say I liked the taste of coffee until I discovered that it could be made differently—the same with tea. I usually only drank tea when I was sick or needed to relax. When I got donuts, I only drank tea or coffee with them if that was what I was craving. Coffee, in my mind, meant just coffee, cream, and sugar. I didn't see any other way of drinking it. How I thought of it made me not want to try any other form of drinking it. My mind was set. It was the same with tea. I didn't want it if it wasn't Lipton Tea with a bit of lemon and sugar. Sometimes we have to change our mindset to change our providence. Our minds can limit the places we can go.

I had heard of the "S" place before, but whenever I listened to that name, all I could hear was "expensive." I just knew that I wasn't paying for whatever they were offering. I couldn't wrap my mind around coffee (regular coffee) being so expensive. Sometimes we formulate these scenarios in our minds that don't even exist. I am already speaking about a product and its costs, and I haven't even tried it. How do I know if the price is worth it? How do I even know if it's expensive if I've never visited? All my mind had formulated was by what I heard through the grapevine. We must stop believing everything we hear because somethings come to strip our exposure and ability to experience life in ways we could never imagine. I was so closed-minded when it came to coffee, but one day, I got a gift card to the "S" place, and it changed my coffee and tea life!

You see, sometimes, we limit ourselves because our minds are limited. Christ died so that anything concerning His people would not be limited. He does so that we might have life in abundance! We take ourselves out of living a good life. Has someone offered another way for you to do something or go somewhere, and your response was, "I can't do that" or "I'd never try that?" Well, I'm here to tell you to step outside the box! By getting your mind out of bondage, you'd be surprised at what you might learn, see, or experience. Tradition never graduates. If we do the same thing in the same way, we will never grow. When I went to the "S" place and got a Caramel Frappe, I was in heaven! I never thought coffee could taste so good. My tasting pallet was immediately enlightened. If they could talk, they'd probably say, "Child, where has this been?!" Lol! I was hooked. Not only that, but they also had other drinks that I enjoyed with my donuts. Look at

God! I went from having coffee one way to having it entirely differently. This happens in our life. Some exposure is alright. God is always trying to get us to learn new ways, and different things, to get us to experience this abundant life He died for. Get out of your way! Live a little.

Honey, even my tea pallet was enlightened. Have you ever had a Medicine Ball from the "S" place? If you haven't, try it. It saved me on days when I had a cold. Here I am, thinking Lipton Tea was it. No ma'am! It Changed my tea game. I'm not sure if I hadn't gotten those gift cards or if I would have ventured off to living an "S" place Coffee/Tea life. God knows what we need; sometimes, it takes someone else to push us in that direction. If you have someone in your corner who is pushing you to go further and see life differently, go for it! The "S" place was my example, but God uses so many things to get us to live a whole and abundant life in Him. The word tells us that the Earth is the Lord's and the fullness thereof. He wants us to have access to everything good that the Earth has to offer.

Move out of the way. Get out of your mind. Break the traditional ways of doing things and step outside of the box. God will never lead you astray and will not hold any good thing from you. Go for it!

*The Earth is the LORD's, and the fulness thereof; The world, and they that dwell therein.* **PSALM 24:1**

# Chapter 15

## Coffee Gone Wild!

Choosing your favorite donut spot might not seem like much to you, but it means a lot To the business owner. It means a lot to them because they know that if their shop is your first choice, you will be faithful in buying their products. It's a win-win situation; you become a loyal customer, and they become an authentic donut supplier. You trust them to remain faithful in providing your product, and they trust you in buying it.

Think about that for a second. What if we become faithful to the Lord like we become faithful to things of this world? If God trusts us, we must prove ourselves trustworthy, just like we trust in Him and expect Him to be faithful. I can't even count the number of times I've frequented my favorite donut shop. It's too many to count! When I visited the shop, I expected them to have what I needed. Sometimes they did, and sometimes they didn't, but God? He has never failed me! When we become faithful to Him, he never lets us down. You hear me... Never! He even keeps us when we are in our folly, but that's another teaching. Just like we make our favorite donut spot our first choice, we should do the same with God. We make Him our first choice, and He becomes our ONLY supplier. It's a Win-Win. We win, and so does the kingdom. He can't trust us when we fail at being faithful to Him; when we try to implement substitutions, we invite problems in.

I remember one day, I pulled up to my favorite donut shop. I saw a truck of someone I knew there, but the truck was parked on the side of the building instead of the front. It baffled me because there were plenty of empty parking spots in front of the door. I just thought it was weird that it looked to be "hidden." I was on my phone when I noticed this person's spouse pull up in their car, but they parked in the front. At this point, I am asking myself why they drove in two separate vehicles when they both lived in the same house. I might have been overthinking it, so I kept doing what I was doing on my phone. Keep in mind that the windows at this shop are see-through like many other shops. A few minutes go by, and As I sat there on my phone, I see cups of ice and coffee flying across the store. A lady's hand is moving aggressively in the air as she is yelling, but I can't hear anything because I am not inside. I can only see the chaos going on in the store. The spouse was there with another person, and their spouse came in and caught them, and that's when coffee and ice started flying.

I didn't see any donuts involved, but that's neither here nor there. I felt awful because I knew these people and started to get out of the car to try and diffuse the situation but to save them the embarrassment, I just stayed in my car and prayed.

Do you see what happens when we need to be more faithful to what we say we will be devoted to? The enemy wreaks havoc! He doesn't care about our feelings, embarrassing us, where he embarrasses us, or anything that protects who we are. His main job is to steal your joy, kill your dreams, and destroy you overall. Here we have a married couple in turmoil because someone opened a portal for the enemy to enter. I noticed that the mistress seemed to have left unharmed and unbothered. She walked out like she was the ultimate prize. The enemy has a way of making us look like fools, and his work looks grand. We have to remain faithful to the things of God because when we do, He provides the strength to deny the temptations that come to bring chaos. I'm sure the mistress thought she had won because she didn't look like the fool then, but she was the fool because that was somebody else's husband. I'm sure she didn't realize it at that moment, but she realized it later. I'm sure she concluded that we can't have something or try to invoke our wants on something God ordained for someone else. You put yourself in a position to be hurt in the end.

Remain faithful to the Lord. In all things. Not just with our relationships but with our life. It's not worth it to lose everything because of diverse temptations. The enemy doesn't have anything to lose, thus the reason why he could care less about what's going to happen to you. He wants to gain your life in the interim. Being faithful to the Lord and everything else will be fine. Keep your coffee in your cup.

No more Coffee Gone Wild!

*Now it is required that those who have been given a trust must prove faithful.* **-1 Corinthians 4:2, NIV**

# Chapter 16

---

## Not A Donut Fan

I am sure that we all know that everyone is not a fan of jelly donuts, and I was never a fan until I came across a Boston crème donut. I know that isn't a jelly donut, but I put them in the same category because of the filling. The Boston Crème donut made me try other "filled" donuts because, before that, it was No, No, No! You couldn't get me to try anything that was filled!

Although I wasn't a jelly donut fan, those around me didn't allow that to influence their decision on what type of donut they liked or wanted. When they ate a jelly donut before I liked them, they didn't push me to try it or force me to eat it. We all had our likes/dislikes, and we were all okay living in our donut spaces.

Sometimes, we think we don't have people's support if they don't like what we are doing. They could be of help, and it might not be the support you are seeking. The fact that they support your sound decision to enjoy what you enjoy is wholesome support, and we don't see that as support; however, if we have family and friends in our circle who allow us to enjoy our uniqueness without judgment or blame, honey, that is support! Especially the things that we do in God.

Sometimes, we think that they don't support us when people aren't doing what we are doing or going where we are going. What would we accomplish if the Lord created us all to go in the same direction, like the same things, and be the same way? So many things would go undone, and it would be a boring world! Thank God, He uniquely created us all, knowing what we needed individually and collectively. He is a God of great detail.

We have to come to the reality that everybody is not going to support our decision. For some of us, God made it that way. He knows who needs to support, who needs to leave, who needs to come, who needs to go, who needs to be a part of it etc. I was not too fond of jelly donuts at first, but somewhere down the line, I started liking them. I might not have supported my family in eating them prior, but eventually, I did. Ultimately, I supported their decision to eat it along with them. There might be a better time for people to support. They might not have the capacity to support during that time. Their posture and support might need to be better intentions. So many things could be, but do not let that influence your decision on what God has for you. If God led you to do something, He has set the proper people to support it. Please don't force it! Be okay with what He has provided and your decision to follow through. Your obedience is the sacrifice that will open doors to proper support.

When we desire to support, we should ensure that it's God-led support. If my family had forced, pushed, and aggravated me about trying a jelly donut, I probably would have never tried it. I would have felt it was being forced upon me rather than deciding to do so. Anything that is forced to receive will have to be forced to be kept. They asked at the beginning, and I Declined. It wasn't a fight. You want God to be amid that support. You also want the heart of those that support it to be upright before God. Otherwise, you force yourself into becoming entangled with the support that could drain you. Support that could Rob you of the joy of doing what you are called to. Unfortunately, sometimes that requires walking alone until God sends your help. I ate plenty of glazed donuts alone until support came (Boston Crème Donut) 😄. There will be many days of feeling alone, but God will be with you.

Everybody will not be a fan of what God has called you to. It's okay. If God is leading you, He won't steer you wrong. He will allow you to run into an awaiting audience ready to receive and assist you along the way. Keep walking. You will find many new things on your journey. You will also find that there will be others who love jelly donuts as much as you do!

*"Be strong and courageous. Do not fear or be in dread of them, for it is the LORD your God who goes with you. He will not leave you or forsake you." -**Deuteronomy 31:6***

# Chapter 17

## Religious Donuts

Several people I know will only buy a particular type of donut. The place doesn't matter. It's all about the product. If they go to Dunkin, Ducks Donuts, or a local bakery, they get the same type of donut every time. They religiously eat the same kind of donut with their coffee, no matter what. Some might see it as boring, but to each their own. No judgment here. There is nothing that can persuade them to try another or that will convince them to step outside of their ordinary. I wouldn't be surprised if God offered them another type of donut, and they denied Him. Lol! However, they have tried many times to convince others that their donut choice was the best. They had no issue trying to get people to try their version. Isn't it ironic how some people don't want you to step outside the norm, but they want you to live in their norm? Go figure!

I've never wondered why they didn't want to venture out and try other donuts, and I assumed that maybe they did and didn't like them, or perhaps they didn't and didn't want to. Either way, it was a decision they made. One they have to live with, and that's okay.

When people make decisions, they have to understand that it is theirs to live with, and others have a choice not to live with it. Sometimes people want you to live in the "norm" because they are. If they haven't been exposed to something different, they don't want you to, either. It could be the fear of the unknown or the fear of experiencing something new. Who knows? Some people live by tradition and don't know any other way but their way. Others are stuck in their way of doing things. As stated previously, tradition never graduates. If we do something the same way for the rest of our lives, there will be no growth. God created us all different but alike in our unique way. Yes, we all can eat the same donut, which makes us alike in that way, but he also made us different because we have an appetite for other things too. Ultimately, it all comes together to acknowledge who he has made us to be. Your donut choices might look different from someone else's. The exposure that your taste buds experience from your choice might be different, and that's fine as long as your choice is God's choice.

We don't all have to be the same, look the same, act the same, etc. God wanted us to step outside the box, think outside the box, and go further than the parameters this world has set for us to be in. We were never created to be boxed in. When he created Adam, Adam was in complete control over where his feet went and had dominion over everything therein. Try new things. Do it another way. Create a new way of doing things. God has given you the gift to do so. Use them! This world is waiting for some of us to come out of our comfort zones and exercise the gifts God has given us. Go for it!

I remember when I started, My Wife Can't Cook and the noise behind it. How could God possibly put His word inside a cooking group? What does food have to do with God's word? God is not in food! "This isn't what God called, and it's not Religious." I mean, the noise went on and on. The noise was so loud it almost made me quit. It almost made me forget why God told me to start it in the first place. His permission was granted, and that's all I needed.

Was it different? Yes. It was very different. It was Unique. It didn't look like anything anyone had seen, but it was GOD. We cannot get stuck in worrying about being like everyone else. What God has for you is for you, and He has created your unique way of doing it. God knew I would have never started a cooking group.

Knowing I can't cook, He had another plan for My Wife Can't Cook. The plan that was never about me, but His people: trust His plan even when it doesn't seem religious, traditional, or similar to what someone else did. If you know for a surety that God led you to do it, Do It!

Think Different. Be Different. Do it Differently. Tradition never Graduates, but obedience does.

*He answered them, "And why do you break the commandment of God for the sake of your tradition? **Matthew 15:3***

# Chapter 18

## Jelly Donuts Don't Talk

J elly donuts don't talk. Some of us don't need to either, lol! They can't say words, have a conversation, or any of the above because they were not created to talk, but just like us, even a jelly donut makes a noise when bitten into.

In a perfect world, we expect people to treat us the way we treat them, love them the way that we love them, and respect us the way we appreciate them. That's in a perfect world and has not been the reality for many of us.

There are many people in this world with good intentions, good motives, and good hearts. If you are one of those people, you cannot allow the actions of those without good intentions to affect who God has created you to be. That includes the times when you are hurt and have every right to retaliate. You still have to keep your character and posture intact no matter what someone does to you. I know that is easier said than done, but it is the character that God requires us to walk in.

69

One of the best ways to keep your composure is silence. From experience, I know that some things warrant a response and the ability for you to defend yourself, but for some people, even that won't matter. If someone has an ill heart toward you, nothing can deliver them from that but God. That's for the saint and the sinner. Our response, whether verbal or through action, will not stop them from being who they want to be. The root of why they are the way they are usually has nothing to do with you. You are just the recipient of the trauma they've never dealt with. We cannot combat flesh with flesh. It won't work. There is nothing to counteract the Spirit that is at work. We must allow God to be our refuge and revenge in those cases. Negative cannot cast out negative. For the problem to resolve, somebody has to do something different. Unfortunately, most of the time, it lands in the hands of the mistreated person.

You see, people misconstrue silence as being weak. Silence during a storm is the epitome of strength. People think of silence; they automatically assume everything is quiet and shut down. They feel that there is no work being done behind the scenes, and they are entirely shutting the person down. The only thing that has become silent is the flesh. The type of silence the Lord is referring to is the kind that shuts our flesh down toward the enemy and activates the Spirit within us. The enemy can only respond to the noise of the flesh. He becomes silent to that of the Spirit because he is not more robust than the Lord. When he thinks we are silent, we aren't. It is just that our flesh is quiet, but our Spirit is speaking loudly. The problem is he can't hear it! We cannot afford to retaliate with our tongue, actions, or posture because that distracts us from what God wants to do through us in the Spirit. As long as we react with our flesh, the noise will never end, the storm will linger, and the enemy will feed and grow from what we give him. That's why he wants our flesh to keep active. As long as it's functional, he can be involved. Silence is getting retaliation through prayer, fasting, reading God's word, and seeking God amid the trial. We strategically place ourselves ahead of the enemy's tactics and ways when we discipline our flesh. While he is raising noise, God is raising an army within us and raising a standard against him.

I remember going through something; by nature, I wanted to pull out receipts, recordings, cuss, disassociate myself, and everything else you could think of, but God told me no. He reminded me who I was, who I belonged to, and what I was a representation of. He explained that the enemy was waiting for me to come out of character to accuse me of being someone I was not. He showed me that he was waiting. He revealed the traps and the plans that he set. He promised he would speak for me, and it would be loudly before those who lied on me, talked about me, and conspired against me. I remember the words so clearly "I am the Lion of Judah, and I will Roar for you!" He stated that I needed to be still.

And silent, and it took all I had to do so. I cried for many days, but it was accompanied by much prayer. I didn't understand what He meant at first, but He revealed later that the enemy scatters just at his roar from a distance. That reassured me that whatever the enemy had planned that was near me or further down the line, God would take care of me Just by his roar! He won't even have to lift a hand. I envisioned a Lion roaring in the wilderness, and when the Lion roars, every creeping enemy runs at the sound of it, even enemies near and far. Oh, what a security that was to my soul!

God will speak for you no matter how hard life gets, what people do, or what they say. Being silent doesn't mean you are weak. It means you are stronger than your enemy, who appears to be more than it is. Silence doesn't mean stagnant. It means working in the Spirit with the Lord to destroy your enemy acting out in the flesh. Be reminded that no matter how hard life bites us, it is not greater than the God within us! Noise from the enemy is but for a moment, but the roar of the Lion of Judah is an eternal sound in Glory.

*But you belong to God, my dear children. You have already won a victory over those people because the Spirit who lives in you is greater than the Spirit who lives in the world.* ***1 John 4:4***

# Chapter 19

## Donut Change

For years I would only eat glazed donuts. That was my signature donut; no one could tell it wasn't the best on the shelf. One reason it was my donut of choice is, that's the kind of donut I grew up on. It was all I knew, but I got older, and my appetite changed.

I remember the very first time I ever tried a Boston Crème Donut. My best friend loves them, and at the time, I didn't know she did. One day we were on the phone, and she mentioned that she had to stop by the donut shop to get her favorite donut. I was inquisitive and wanted to know what type of donut she liked. She began to tell me how good this Boston Crème donut was. The way she explained it made me want to get one delivered ASAP. My mouth was drooling as she was describing it. Her persuasion of how great this donut was truly mesmerizing! So much so that I went and got one as soon as we hung up.

I remember going into the donut shop, ordering it, and being scared to try something new. I was wondering if I would like it when

I saw what it looked like and ordered a glazed donut, too, to be safe. Sometimes, fear will make you revert to the old when God is trying to introduce the new. I got back home and tried the donut, and honey, I was hooked! I loved the chocolate and crème combination. Those flavors danced in my mouth like a fish in freshwater!

Change is sometimes good. Many of us tend not to go outside the box, especially when we don't know what's outside. I grew up on glazed donuts. It was all I knew, so it was my choice by default. That happens to many of us. How we were raised tends to affect how we live as adults, whether good, bad, or indifferent. When God introduces something better or new, it can seem uncomfortable because it's outside what we are used to. He could be trying to change your appetite. When your appetite changes, it exposes you to greater and better. That can be scary when you don't know what better looks like. It forces you to step out in faith, trusting God knows what's best for you. His word is an excellent tool of persuasion that convinces you that He will be with you every step of the way. You will find that the change He introduces is for a moment and a lifetime.

Embracing Change is a good thing, but with Change, you have to let some things go. I'm trying a new donut. I had to let go of the idea that glaze was the only good donut. I found out that it wasn't. Although that was something I learned from childhood, that didn't mean it was true. Often, we grow up hearing and learning things that aren't necessarily true. This also happens in the church. When you cultivate your relationship with God, change occurs in every area of your life. Your mind. You begin to think differently—your heart. You begin to love differently—your soul. You begin to live differently. It exposes you to the truth of who He is and the falsehood of what you might have learned. Some of us have to unlearn things to change. One of the most challenging things to do while discovering Change is Unlearning and Learning simultaneously. It's hard to break old habits, but with God, it can be done successfully.

Embrace Change. Embrace everything that comes along with it. Feel free to go to new places, try new things, think more extensively, and do big things. God is trying to push you out of your comfort zone, and being uncomfortable will take you places that being comfortable never will. Embrace Change and allow God to lead you in all things. Go ahead and try that donut you've never tried! Change is Good, and you might love it!

*You were taught, about your former way of life, to put off your old self, which is being corrupted by its deceitful desires; to be made new in the attitude of your minds; and to put on the new self, created to be like God in true righteousness and holiness. ---**Ephesians 4:22-24***

# Chapter 20

## Painful Jelly

Donuts are quick, sweet, and scrumptious snacks available to anyone who can purchase one. However, just because we can doesn't mean we should. Everything that appears to look good isn't always good for you.

If you are an individual with an underlying condition such as diabetes, high blood pressure, high cholesterol, etc., a donut might not be a good snack for you. Although you can purchase one doesn't mean that you should due to the underlying conditions you have. Eating a donut can cause you more harm than good.

Think about our lives. How many of us have underlying conditions that we override to have something our flesh desires for a moment? How many of us have daddy issues that we haven't dealt with, and we enter into a relationship looking for a daddy in our spouses? How many of us have mother issues, get into a relationship, and look to our wives as mothers? Whenever there is an underlying issue that isn't dealt with properly, it can cause more damage. I remember having father issues. I grew up without my natural father and only dealt with him after marriage. My husband and I met when we were still very young, but I remember the difficulty in separating the Father from the Husband (he was my boyfriend then). I didn't realize it until we moved into our first apartment. I had been looking to him to father me rather than being my partner. The underlying issue had introduced itself in our relationship. It was challenging since he was doing many things for me that a father would do. Although he was seemingly filling that role, I had to realize that he was serving the role as my partner and not as my father. The issue was so deeply rooted that they looked very similar. I had to Go to the Lord and ask Him to help me separate the two. It was too hard for me to handle alone. Eventually, it dissolved, but the underlying issue of not having a father caused more harm than good.

Understand that when we purchase the donut, even though we should not, the consequences of that purchase will eventually show up. We have to ensure that we are not incubators for harmful bacteria. It stays hidden until a situation that can feed off it presents itself. We often move forward as if we have overcome the issue until we are in a position and that thing plays peek-a-boo in our life. Like, hey, I'm still here! Frequently, it affects and infects relationships that we have with people. We must confront it, or else bacteria will grow and cause self-inflicted wounds. We also cannot expect our partner or the person we are in a relationship with to accept our bacteria. It's almost like trying to make someone share your disease. That's insane! If they are in a relationship with you, they are subject to the same bacteria, and that Spirit can also attach itself to them if they aren't strong enough in the Spirit. We have to address it. When we do, it is beneficial to all parties involved. Taking the mindset of "that's just how I am" is a cowardly excuse for not wanting to CHANGE. Most times, the people experiencing the bacteria's side effects had nothing to do with it being there, yet they've become recipients of the residue of it. They weren't there. They had nothing to do with it, so we cannot make them pay the penalty for something they weren't a part of. When the Lord revealed that to me in my relationship with my husband, it hit hard, but it was what I needed to break that cycle and move forward.

Change can be difficult, but it's necessary. Sometimes we make things more complicated than they need to be, and God makes things simple. We are the ones who complicate things. Welcome change and welcome your healing. Proceed with caution. Address the hidden condition before entering something new to prevent further damage. You got this!

*Not only so, but we also glory in our sufferings because we know that suffering produces perseverance; perseverance, character; and character, hope. And hope does not put us to shame because God's love has been poured out into our hearts through the Holy Spirit, who has been given to us. -**Romans 5:3-5***

# Chapter 21

❧

## Fraternal Donuts

Some stores carry those dual-pack donuts that you can buy. Most of the time, they are the same type of donut. (2) glazed or (2) Boston Creme etc. You rarely find a box with two different kinds of donuts. I like to call them Fraternal Donuts.

Although the donuts are in the same pack, one of the donuts has to leave the package to be eaten. As soon as the "chosen" one leaves the pack and is bitten into, they are no longer "twin donuts" because one was eaten. Just imagine that for a moment. How many of us went into something, whether with a family member, a friend, a partner, etc., but one of the two was chosen for a specific assignment and had to leave the "pack?"

I think there is a great misconception, especially within families, that families must be together or stick together to accomplish what God has called them to do. That is not true! Honestly, everybody, even family, will not go where you go. Some don't have the desire or the mentality to go or grow. Sometimes the guilt of wanting them to grow or do better can become a weight on you and make you carry a weight you were never meant to carry. It can stop movement in the right direction altogether. We have to understand what God has called us to individually and collectively, and unfortunately, even family won't understand your assignment. They won't appreciate your press or your journey. You have to be careful for those of you who have big hearts and are willing to carry and help people. Family can drain and abuse the gift of "giving." Start saying no, and you will see who remains and who goes. Christ Himself said in His word, "Who is My Mother, and who are my brothers? For whoever does my father's will is my brother, sister, and mother."

Many of us come from the same blood, but the blood that is "running" might not be the same. You might come from a place of Love and Respect, and they might come from a place of Abuse and Manipulation. These types of blood are different. One holds the attributes of God, and the other contains a quality of an opposing force. Sometimes we forget that the enemy comes for blood too, and he comes to taint the blood that God has provided for us.

People grow apart. What will happen when God chooses you for a journey separate from those you are used to being around? You have to have enough confidence to step out in God, which means in faith, trusting that God will see you through. It's tough to leave some behind, but if they aren't willing to grow, are you going to stay behind? I know it's a tough decision, but it's a decision that can be accomplished with God's instruction.

We all have relationships, partnerships, and connections that we grow apart from. Never feel guilty for what He has chosen you to do. We all have different journeys; if your family loves you, they will support you even if they aren't going along. That is true love!

*While Jesus was still talking to the crowd, His mother and brothers stood outside, wanting to speak to Him. Someone told Him, "Your mother and brothers are standing outside, wanting to speak to you."*
**Matthew 12:46-48**
*He replied to him, "Who is my mother, and who are my brothers?"*

# Chapter 22

## One of A Kind

If you visit donut shops frequently, you will notice that most of the time, they have mini versions of each type of donut they have. If they have big-powered donuts, they have mini powdered donuts. There is usually no difference between the two but the size. Whatever ingredients the big donut was made of, most likely, the mini donut was made out of the same thing. It's just a smaller amount of it. They are almost one of a kind.

For those of you who have children, you will be able to relate to the things that will be pinned in this chapter, and by now, you probably have an inkling of where I am going with this message. If you are a parent who has dealt with trauma and has difficulty overcoming it, most of the time, our little ones have dealt with it too. When trauma introduces itself during pregnancy, the baby feels the brunt of the pain. They can sense when the mother feels defeated, oppressed, and stressed, amongst many other things happening outside and inside the womb. As parents, we must set boundaries early on so that our children do not become subject to the trials we've

82

experienced. I can relate. As a child, I suffered many traumas not of my own but from my parent's experiences.

Although I was not the one it was directed to, the remnant of that trauma fell on me by default. When the trauma was evident, I heard the abuse and saw it; therefore, it made me become just as traumatized by the situation as the parent going through it. Our children will not know how to handle the trauma if we have not figured out how to handle it. So, in turn, the parent and the child struggle together. The difference in the struggles is that the parent can identify where the trauma stems from, but usually, the bystander can only determine what they see by the surface. They have no idea what the root of the matter is. It forces them to mature quickly to fight a spirit much more skilled than they are. They are children and some of the things they become subject to are unfair.

In their minds, they want to protect and love, so they exercise that in their flesh, not realizing it's a spiritual fight. As parents, sometimes we send them to war without any garments. We must adequately handle our trauma, whether with the Lord, through Therapy, or by Leaving the situation altogether. We have to do whatever is best for their well-being. Otherwise, that same truth will show up in our Children. Some act out in school, withdraw, become promiscuous, disrespectful, etc. That is because whatever spirit was at work where there was no standard, the spirit had full reign. It not only came to do damage but to do collateral damage to try and destroy whatever greatness and gift God has for that child.

As I write this, I am in tears because I am guilty of passing trauma to my children. Not directly or purposely, but they received the remnants of my pain. I didn't realize it until my oldest was in her teens. I remember having a family meeting, and she voiced how I wasn't there emotionally for her. It broke my heart to hear her say those words, but it was true. I didn't realize that due to the trauma I had been through, I became numb to certain emotions because people had become numb to mine. I figured I didn't have to address the pain if I didn't feel it. If I didn't address other people's emotions, they didn't have to address mine. I didn't want any parts because of the noise and hurt I witnessed as a child. My parent was a great parent. I believe they did their best with what they were dealt with, but emotionalism wasn't a part of my rearing, so it was very foreign to me. I wasn't a hugger. I didn't say I Love you a lot. If someone cried, I quickly tried to dismiss their feelings, etc. I had never confronted that trauma until my daughter mentioned it. Progression started that day.

I began to think back over the years that these trials had affected my relationship with my husband and children, and I must've cried for days. I started praying and asking God how at the age I was, I could fix it. I thought to myself; my daughter is raised now. Is it too late?! I had all of these questions for God and voiced them to Him loudly. I needed this spirit gone and gone now! I didn't want the "one of a kind" mentality to be in my home any longer. The big and the little opposing forces had to cease. I was done! God answered and gave me specific instructions and little by little. I began to plant seeds in my children's lives. I had to do it His way because God knows I didn't know where to start. Is it perfect? No. However, it's better. It was rough initially because that spirit had been exposed, and the adversary was hot (as he should be, hell is hot!), but I could not go on defense those times. I went on offense instead, and it worked. I connected with their feelings, and they received it well during those times. To God be All the Glory!

Parents, address the trauma so your kids won't have to look in the mirror and see you. God has given them their own identities. They need to see themselves and not our trauma. They need to be able to live freely, fulfilling their purpose and not fighting through ours to get to their own. It's too heavy for them to carry. Nobody lifts heavy weights without a spotter. Some of these children carry the consequences of our decisions as weights, crushing their spirits. Our job is to ensure that we build upon what God has already established, not help break it down. I know this can be heavy, but we all must face and confront it. We have to take accountability for the negative influences that we have had in our children's lives. It starts first with acknowledging that you had a part in it. Don't allow Pride to be your portion during the relationship resolution. Instead, embrace the breaking that God is doing and move forward. It's a beautiful thing!

I want you to touch and agree that we will do our best not to have our "mini donuts" emulating the trauma of the "bigger donuts."

The transfer of it stops today. Be blessed and be encouraged. With God, it is possible!

*The eternal God is your refuge,*
*and underneath is the everlasting arms.*
*He will drive out your enemies before you,*
*saying, 'Destroy them!'* **Deuteronomy 33:27**

# Chapter 23

---❦---

## Oh, What A Mess!

I love going to some of the donut shops, and the donuts are sitting on the shelves, all nice and pretty. I am a little OCD, so the way they are set up, nice, and neat makes me happy. The powdered jelly donuts sat nicely with no powder on the shelves or other donuts, and they only appeared messy once you bought them.

I remember buying one and taking a bite out of it, and the jelly from the inside plopped right on the front of my shirt. Boy, was I hot! I must admit, I wasn't eating it like a lady, either. I was devouring it and made a mess of it. On the shelf, it didn't look that messy, but the inside of that thing was very messy. So much jelly!

How many of us are that way? All nice and put together on the outside, but the inside all tore up and messy. How many of us have hair, clothes, and shoes in place, but our inside is all discombobulated? I must admit I was once that way. Just messy. A whole hot mess! God cleaned me up something good.

I used to think that getting my hair done, wearing nice things, and looking a certain way would help me with what I was dealing with inside. Nope! It was just the opposite. When I became cleaned up from the inside, it helped my outside tremendously. Most of the time, when we are messy on the inside, it comes out through our hearts. You see, the word tells us that out of our hearts flows the issues of life. Whatever we are dealing with on the inside will tell on itself when we speak. It will also come out through our actions. It's very difficult to hide. As women, sometimes we can be very aggressive and cantankerous with our tongues due to some things we might have been through. The hurt and the pain introduce themselves in our actions and speech because we speak from a place of pain rather than a place of purpose. Messy! Sometimes we don't even know that we are doing it. Because it has been living there for quite some time, it turns into bitterness and reveals itself in social settings, relationships, friendships, etc. We sometimes even try to recruit other people to come into connection with our messiness by playing the victim instead of exercising being the victor. One of the reasons some of us are messy is because of the chaotic environments we grew up in. Not many of us grew up seeing healthy relationships amongst other women, not to mention healthy marriages. It's a lot to take in!

I met my husband very young. When I look back on our relationship, I went in with good intentions, but things got messy somewhere along the way. It was mainly because of the fear of the relationship failing because I hadn't seen too many (at the time) make it. I began to put up walls to protect myself (just in case) things didn't work. I became messy. I started lashing out all the time. I was becoming aggressive in my tone and talk. It was like I was expecting it to fail when he had not given me a reason that it would. Again, I was basing it on my surroundings instead the standard God set for my marriage. We don't even realize we are becoming messy because that's all we saw. When we recognize it, we have to seek God's help. Some of us may need to add Therapy to the equation to have healthy relationships with people. Once I realized it, I sought God for help. I also had a woman who took me aside and helped me along the way. My mom and mother-in-love(s) (I have two) helped me immensely.

Being messy is not cute and nothing to brag about. When I discovered how messy I was, I was Like, Lord, is it me you want because this is a mess! I was tired of myself after a point. Thank God for Jesus, who is a cleaning expert. He is so gracious and such a good father. When you are all cleaned up, you don't even look like what you have been through. I can now say that God has done work from the inside out. I can proudly get my hair done, nails, etc., and know that I am whole and healed in Him. It is such a liberating and incredible feeling.

No more mess!

*Create in me a clean heart, O God, and renew a right spirit fwithin me.* **Psalm 51:10**

www.ingramcontent.com/pod-product-compliance
Lightning Source LLC
Chambersburg PA
CBHW070441130626
46553CB00006B/2272